WARNING! MANY OF THESE WALKS USE CLIFF PATHS AND ARE DANGEROUS. CHILDREN AND DOGS MUST BE SUPERVISED AT ALL TIMES. ADULTS SHOULD BE VIGILENT, NOT ONLY FOR THEMSELVES BUT FOR ANYONE WHO IS WITH THEM

WALKS
ON THE
YORKSHIRE COAST

by

J.Brian Beadle

INTRODUCTION

Walking on Yorkshire's coastal paths can be a dangerous pastime for the unwary. Please be extra vigilant whilst walking these paths, especially if you have children or animals with you. Some of the paths can be slippery when wet, some may have fallen into the sea after a winter storm whilst others may be well cared for by voluntary organisations. An offshore wind blowing at 10 m.p.h. when you leave home is probably building up to nearer 20 m.p.h. as it races out into the open sea from the cliff top.

When walking on the beach have respect for the tide, it is so easy to be cut off. Please take care, go well prepared taking with you warm waterproof clothing, food, water and the old favourites, map, compass and whistle.

You might wonder when the old fools going to stop bleating about safety! As long as you heed the warnings he'll say no more!

Some of the walks have a strong historical theme to them. The old smugglers haunts can be fascinating. Try imagining what it would be like dodging the excise man on a moonless night along the Bolts at Scarborough or Robin Hoods Bay, with a barrel of Brandy on your shoulder.

Picture the scene at Ravenscar when the flat bottomed ships edged their way onto the beach with a stinking cargo of urine for company. Then the sweating and toiling of men who were needed to haul it up the cliff. There was much mining activity along this part of the coast extracting clay, shale and jet. Today, activity is in the leisure trade as walkers and cyclists explore the old paths along the coast.

Before setting out on any of these routes I recommend that you consult the appropriate Ordnance Survey map for detail. The maps in the book are only a guide to the rights of way.

I'm sure you will enjoy walking along the coast of North Yorkshire.

J. Brian Beadle

1994
Revised 2002

ISBN 189900405X

INDEX

ROUTE 1

OLD STAITHES

*S*taithes *is situated in a deep, rugged creek 10 miles north west of Whitby. The main industry at Staithes is fishing. Many years ago fish that was to be cured was cut up & salted, brined, then laid out on the beach to dry. In the early nineteenth century fifteen cobbles would have been engaged in the Herring industry. There were around 400 men and boys engaged in the fishing industry at Stathes.*

Runswick Bay is a very scenic place. There are caves where the sea has washed holes in the rock. Like Staithes, fishing is prominent but perhaps is now surpassed by the leisure industry.

FACT FILE

Distance - 7 miles (11km)
Time - 3 hours
Grading - Easy
Map - OS Landranger 101
Start - Runswick Bay. GR 807162.
Parking - Large car park at Runswick Bay.
Refreshments - Runswick Bay & Staithes. The Fox & Hounds at Dalehouse.

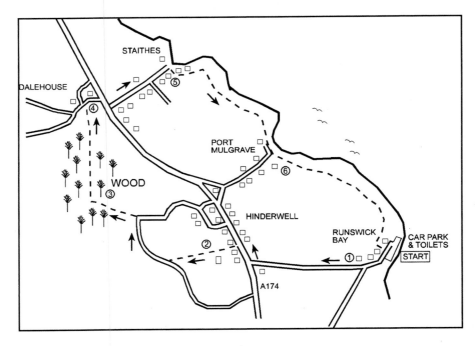

THE ROUTE

1. Start from the clifftop car park at Runswick Bay. Do not go down the hill into the old village it is better to park at the top and walk down later. Leave the park and take the road left to Hinderwell. Rejoin the A 174 at the war memorial in Hinderwell. Bear right into the village, then in about 50 yards cross the road and walk along a lane between house numbers 98 & 100.

2. Continue along past the school to a stile. Follow the track across the field then exit right onto a sometimes muddy lane. Follow the lane until it bends back towards the village. Do not follow the lane to the village but take the stile on the left into a field. Crossing the field brings you to another stile to take you downhill into a wood and a stream. Cross the footbridge and take the path uphill into a field and turn right.

3. Walk along the side of the field and at the corner of the field turn right into the wood. Be careful not to miss this turn! In the wood take the path to the left. Keep on this path for some time as it winds its way through the wood until you reach a junction of tracks. Go straight ahead here onto a wider path passing the sign for the Oak Ridge Nature Reserve. Continue on for a short while to a gate leaving the wood. Eventually down a steep hill to another gate into a caravan site.

4. Continue through the caravan site turning right over a wooden bridge, finally taking the dirt road on the left to take you to Dalehouse. At Dalehouse turn right past the Fox & Hounds to exit onto the A174. Go right for a few yards then cross the road to turn left to walk to Staithes old village.

5. Down the steep hill now into another world, the old houses and shops that haven't changed in a hundred years. Continue along through quaint old streets to the harbour where you will find the Cod & Lobster pub. Turn right along Church Street here to ascend the cobbled road and then steps to take you to the cliff top.

6. Follow the Cleveland Way signs to the left then an obvious path all the way along the cliffs to Port Mulgrave. Take to the road here for a short while then when it bends to the right, rejoin the cliff path to the left past some large boulders. Continue along the cliff until you see a sign pointing inland for Runswick Bay. Turn right here and follow the path to the road then left to the car park.

There are fine viewpoints along the cliffs between Runswick Bay and Staithes. To the north is the Boulby potash mine which reaches out under the sea and is the deepest mine in the country. The cliffs at Boulby are the highest cliffs in England and are a stimulating site from any angle.

ROUTE 2

MULGRAVE WOODS

T his walk through Mulgrave Woods is steeped in history and folklore. The focal point of the walk, the old castle, was probably built in Saxon times and is a crumbling but proud monument to its former glory. There have been three castles in the woods at Mulgrave. The Marquis of Normanby lives in today's castle which was built in the 18th century. But apart from the one which you are to visit there was another Mulgrave Castle built on an adjacent ridge by a Saxon Duke called Wada. Or was it the giant Wade who is said to have roamed these parts hundreds of years ago? My vote goes to the Saxon, but the giants tales are entertaining and add a flavour to the walk. Wada's castle would have been made from wood and only the Motte remains. It is on the adjacent ridge to the walk but is accessible from the Lythe - Ugthorpe road.

FACT FILE.
Distance - 3½ miles (6km)
Time - 1½ hours
Grading - Easy
Map - OS Landranger 94
Start - Sandsend. GR 239720
Refreshments - Sandsend

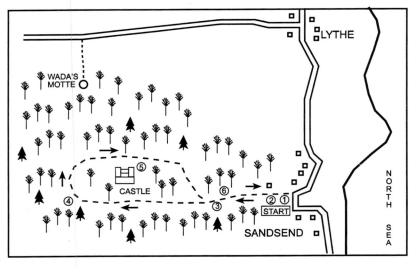

THE ROUTE

1. The walk starts in the village of Sandsend. There is ample parking on the road. Alternatively there is a small car park at the entrance to Mulgrave Woods. When approaching from Whitby enter Sandsend carefully, for where the road does a 'U-turn' over a narrow bridge you must turn sharp left if using the car park.

2. The Woods are only open on Wednesdays, Saturdays and Sundays, and not at all during the month of May. Enter the woods through the gate at the rear of the car park. Follow the path by the river side until it reaches the sawmill. Go through the mill yard and exit through a gate close to the bungalow on the right.

3. The woods have a mixture of deciduous and evergreen trees with a generous sprinkling of wild flowers in the undergrowth.
When the path splits bear right. In fact keep bearing right each time there is a choice of route, except at the tunnel. Do not take the tunnel path at this stage. Eventually the path makes a rising 'U-turn' to the right. The path now becomes a little more overgrown and muddy underfoot but you are almost at the entrance to the castle.

4. At the top of the rise the overgrown stone walls of the early Mulgrave Castle loom into view, an impressive sight! Please read the notices on entering the Castle grounds as the structure of the walls are rather precarious. The huge mullioned window is still intact. What a magnificent place this must have been!

5. Keep the Castle ruins on the right to exit at the diagonally opposite corner to which you arrived and drop down onto a path, turning left. At the clearing keep right. This path eventually joins the one you came on and takes you back to the car park at Sandsend.

6. If you have time to spare on the way back you will find plenty of other paths to ramble about on and you may now explore through the tunnel! But do not venture too far or you will reach the new Mulgrave Castle which is the seat of the Marquis of Normanby.

Mulgrave Castle is believed to have been built by the powerful family of Mauley and it was supposedly founded in Saxon times. In 1773 it was occupied by one Captain Phipps who led an expedition to the North Pole. Today, the ruins stand proud, if a little frail.

THE RUINS OF MULGRAVE CASTLE

ROUTE 3

SEARCHING FOR A KIPPER!

*N*o walking book on the east coast would be complete without a visit to Whitby and the consuming of one or more pairs of Fortune's oak smoked kippers! Where is Fortune's? On Henrietta Street. Where is Henrietta Street? Well, by the time that you visit it could well be in the harbour! The cliff is being undermined in the area and at the far end of the street serious erosion has taken place although restoration work is now in place giving access to the far pier again. I have titled this walk 'searching for a kipper' but it could easily have been called 'looking for a Fortune'!

FACT FILE.
Distance - 3 miles (5km)
Time - 2½ hours (Plus finding the Kipper time)
Grading - Easy
Map - A Street Map of Whitby would be useful
Start - Whitby Abbey car park
Grid Reference - 905113
Refreshments - Abundant at Whitby. Try the Shepherds Purse at the rear of the shop or Botham's in Skinner Street above the shop

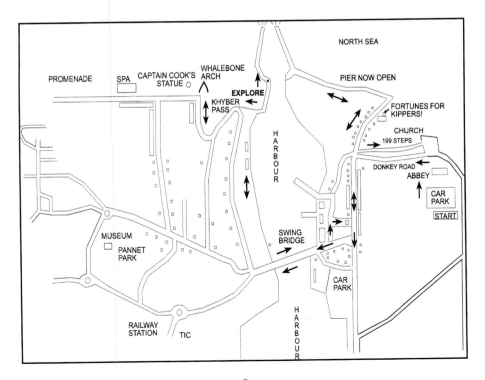

Approach the Abbey car park from the A171 Scarborough to Whitby road. Now would be a good time to explore the Abbey, Church and Visitor Centre.

THE ABBEY
The original Abbey built on the headland was probably of wood and housed both nuns and monks. It was set up by the Abbess Hilda in 657AD. It was here that Caedmon, a young, shy farm worker became a poet and writer of songs. One night whilst he was asleep in the stable with the animals he had a vision calling on him to sing the beginning of created things. His retiring disposition deserted him and he sang about the creation of the world and the origin of man. He sang about the last judgement and the pains of hell comparing it with the delights of heaven. In AD870 the Abbey was destroyed by Danish raiders, only to be rebuilt again by William de Percy around the 11th century. The magnificent ruin to be seen at Whitby today has suffered badly over the years. A terrible storm in December 1763 felled the western wing, then in June 1830 part of the massive central tower collapsed. In the great storm of January 1839 the wind blew down the south wall. Not only did it have to contend with the elements but the German Navy bombarded Whitby in 1914. The front of the Abbey was hit as was the west door. The building is now looked after by English Heritage and is open virtually all year round.

ST. MARY'S CHURCH
This is the Parish Church of Whitby and stands on the lofty east cliff adjacent to the Abbey ruins. Some parts are thought to be older in origin than the Abbey itself but it has undergone lots of alterations in its lifetime. It was renovated and enlarged in 1821, 1822 and 1823 and has a capacity for 2000 worshippers. The tower at the west end contains six excellent bells.
In one corner of the burial ground you will find the Caedmon Memorial Cross. It stands twenty feet high and has some superb carvings and inscriptions on all sides. The inscription reads 'To the glory of God and in memory of Caedmon, the father of English sacred song. Fell asleep hard by, 680.'

THE ROUTE
Enough of history, you came here looking for a Fortune and I am sure you will find one, even if it is a little fishy! Walk down the steps past the church (or take the old Donkey road alongside) and keep straight on at the bottom through the old part of Whitby. You will pass some olde worlde shoppes and the olde market square. Stop for a coffee at The Shepherds Purse on the left, you won't be disappointed! At the end of the street turn right to the swing bridge. On the left just before the bridge is Grape Lane and the museum. It is here that the famous explorer James Cook spent his apprenticeship. Cross the bridge and turn right towards the fish pier.
By now you will have passed many shops selling kippers but they are not Fortune's. By the way, you passed the entrance to Henrietta Street some time ago! Did you spot it?

You may now explore the pier and the old lighthouse. Look out for the Khyber Pass road on the left which takes you up to the West Cliff if you wish to visit the Whalebone Arch and Captain Cooks Monument. Explore the long pier and the harbour if you want to, but now it is time to go in search of the Kipper!

Retrace your steps along the fish pier, cross the swing bridge and make your way back to the steps and Donkey road leading to the Abbey.

STOP!

Do not proceed up the steps or onto the Donkey road but take to the street on the left, Henrietta Street, raise your nose into the air and sniff. Follow the smell of smouldering oak and tar mixed with a fishy pong! At the end of the row of houses on the right you will find a Fortune. The old wooden shop and smoke house belonging to the Fortune family is open for the sale of wonderful Kippers. If the smoke house in not in the actual process of smoking ask for a look in, you will be amazed! I will say no more except that you must buy a pair of Kippers, take them home and cook them lightly with care. I will guarantee you will never have eaten a Kipper more tasty, meaty or delicious than a Fortune's oak smoked Kipper. But the pong is another story!

Now that the cliff stabalisation project is complete (2001) take a walk past Fortunes and down the steep path onto the pier. This will give you another aspect of Whitby and a different view of the high cliffs. If you look over the wall on the sea side of the pier you will notice that there is a bypass for the waves to run into. There is the same at the side of the opposite pier. The idea is that when a rough sea is running it protects the harbour allowing the sea to lose some of its force into these channels.

The Herring - the silver darlings of the sea

The Herring industry, and thus the Kipper, conjures up the thrill of the catch to me. As they swarm in huge shoals looking for food the fishermen have easy pickings. Their nets full to bursting with wriggling silver bodies as they haul the little darlings aboard.

The Herring fishery on this coast was of little importance until 1833 when the Whitby Herring Company was formed for the purpose of curing Herrings and other fish for home consumption and exportation. A curing house was built at Tate Hill. In 1840 the quantity of Herrings taken each season was estimated at 800 lasts, half of which were purchased by vessels from France & Belgium. Many were sold fresh in the town and about 120 lasts were cured here and at Staithes, Runswick Bay and other small coastal villages.

Alas, most Kippers today are '
ing session purely for profit. Unlike Fortune's Kippers which are cured by smoke alone giving them that unique flavour and texture that only an entirely oak smoked Kipper can retain.

Herring caught off the Yorkshire coast start their feeding season in May further north as plankton becomes plentiful. Through August and September Herring fishing is in full swing as the shoals move south to eventually reach France and Belgium. It was not only local boats that joined in the harvest of the sea but boats from Cornwall shared in this profitable venture. There was a varying array of boats of different design as they set sail from Scarborough, Whitby, Staithes and other east coast harbours.

The fish were gutted on the quay side by Scottish fisher lasses who followed the boats down the coast. Their skill with the knife was legendary.

All this work and industry to satisfy our desire for the succulent kipper, caught, gutted, sold/bought and taken to the smoke house to be cured. A delicacy that makes my mouth water as I write these words. How did you guess that I love kippers?

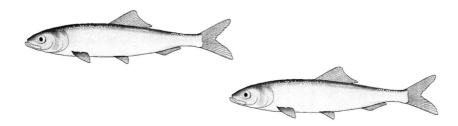

THE UNHAPPY HERRING!

SMUGGLERS AND BOGGLES
A low tide walk

*S*muggling contraband was rife around the coasts of Britain years ago and the people of east Yorkshire were second to none in their efforts to evade the excise man. Robin Hoods Bay hasn't changed much since those tough days. The houses still lean on each other as they cling to the cliff. The sea still pounds against the defences, shaking the foundations of these old houses. Some still have their interconnecting doors and passages through which many a bale of silk or barrel of the finest French Brandy was transported away from suspecting eyes. It is said that it was possible to travel from the sea to the moor using these secret passages without being seen. As you walk around explore some of the old ginnels and alleys. You will find strange names commemorating something or someone from the past. See if you can find Tommy Baxter Street, The Bolts, Jim Bell's Stile and Martin's Row.

FACT FILE.

Distance - 4 miles (5½km)
Time - 2 hours
Grading - Easy
Map - OS Landranger 94. OS Outdoor Leisure 27
Start - Car park at Robin Hoods Bay, grid ref. 952052
Refreshments - A good choice of pubs and cafes in Robin Hoods Bay

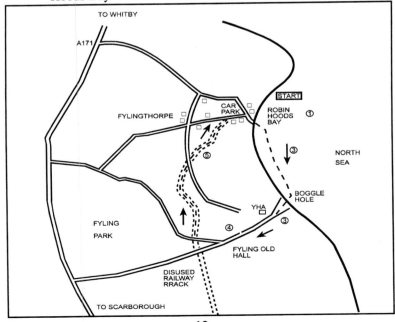

12

THE ROUTE

WARNING! *This route traverses the sea shore and is not passable with an advancing tide. Please allow at least half an hours brisk walking time on the shore. Take the trouble to check the time of high tide before setting off. Heed this warning as the cliffs are subject to erosion and there is no escape!* ***DO NOT RISK BEING CUT OFF BY THE TIDE!!***

1. The walk starts from Robin Hoods Bay a couple of miles off the A171 Scarborough to Whitby road. Park in the old railway station car park in the village and make your way towards the old town down the very steep hill to the beach then turn right along the shore.

2. If you take time to explore the sea shore you might find a piece of jet. Jet is fossilised wood and is worked and polished to make fine jewellery which was so popular with the Victorians. The jet industry was big business in the area around the time of Queen Victoria. Jet is only found on this stretch of the coast.

3. Leave the beach at the first inlet on the right, Boggle Hole. The curious name of Boggle is a Yorkshire name for a Hobgoblin, a mischievous little fellow that used to inhabit these parts! You will see a YHA here. Leave by the road up a steep hill and continue along until the road forks.

4. Take the left fork over a stone bridge crossing the Scarborough to Whitby railway track. Cross the bridge then take the cow path immediately on the right to access the railway track. The track soon crosses a road to scramble up the other side.

5. The track takes you back to the start in a couple of miles. At the road turn right and soon you will come to the car park on your left. Unless you are going to explore the ginnels and alleys and perhaps sample the ale at the Laurel Inn!

- - - o 0 o - - -

The Scarborough to Whitby Railway was given the axe many years ago. The scenic route ferried holiday makers and freight too & fro at regular intervals. The line to the station at the 600ft high Ravenscar station was steep and a special engine was developed, called the 'Whitby Willie', to cope with the incline.
If you listen carefully on a still day you can still hear the engine labouring up the slope belching steam and smoke as it struggles to pull its coaches crammed full of 'mucky-faced' children clutching bucket and spades on their way to Scarborough. Honestly!

ROUTE 5

BIRDS, SHIPS AND LIGHTHOUSES - A WALK AROUND SPURN HEAD

Spurn head is a nature reserve owned by the Yorkshire Wildlife Trust. It is a resting place for migrating birds attracting bird watchers from all over the country. The headland of Spurn is a continuously shifting spit of land. As the erosion of the coast further north provides silt to build a new spit it in turn causes the erosion of the existing peninsula. Each time a new spurn point is built by the sea it is a little further west than the pervious one.

A monastery was built here in 670 and in the late 1200's there was a town, a chapel and even a member of parliament. However the sea was obviously not of the same political leaning and washed it away in 1360.

Lighthouses have been a than ten have been built and either washed away or moved as the spit collapsed and then rejuvenated itself. Today's lighthouse was built between 1893 and 1895, but the remains of the pervious one built in 1852 still stands, alas without its lantern. You will find it resting in the mud in the Humber estuary.

A Humber lifeboat being one of the most famous in the country. Looking along the Humber estuary to the ships slowly creeping their way into the ports further up the river and the sandbanks all around I think the lifeboat will be needed for some time to come. Unless washed away when the sea reclaims the spit in a winters storm!

AN OLD SPURN LIGHTHOUSE

FACT FILE
Distance - 6 miles (10km)
Time - 3 hours walking. Allow more time for exploring.
Grading - Easy
Map - OS Landranger 113
Start - Entrance to Spurn or Spurn car park (fee).
Refreshments - Small cafe run by the lifeboat crew.
When available take the chance to buy a Crab
or Lobster on the point. Follow the sign displayed.

THE ROUTE

It is advisable to walk this route when the tide is out. Starting from the Blue Bell Visitor Centre car park follow the Spurn Footpath way markers towards the cliff top. On the way you will pass a sea watching hide and a bird observatory. Follow the path unless erosion has taken place when you might have to walk on the road or beach. When approaching the lighthouse the path splits. Go left here where there should be a sign saying 'Seaside Path'. This will take you round the headland on the beach after passing the lighthouse. Once round the headland the path goes underneath the jetty then to the Spurn car park. Walk in the direction of the sign for Riverside Footpath then the Spurn Footpath markers will take you back to the Visitor Centre. Alternatively you could visit the Yorkshire Wildlife Trust shop then walk back on the road. If you would like to just potter and only do the short walk around the head you must park on the Spurn car park. Cross the road and walk over the sand dune to the beach, turn right to walk around the headland and return to the car park under the jetty on the riverside path.

If you would like refreshment the cafe is past the car park towards the head on the road, but I cannot guarantee it will be open!

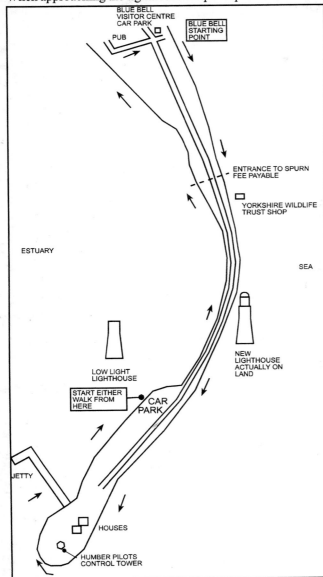

BLUE BELL VISITOR CENTRE CAR PARK
BLUE BELL STARTING POINT
PUB
ENTRANCE TO SPURN FEE PAYABLE
YORKSHIRE WILDLIFE TRUST SHOP
ESTUARY
SEA
NEW LIGHTHOUSE ACTUALLY ON LAND
LOW LIGHT LIGHTHOUSE
START EITHER WALK FROM HERE
CAR PARK
JETTY
HOUSES
HUMBER PILOTS CONTROL TOWER

ROUTE 6

THE RAVENSCAR ROAM

*R*avenscar's heritage includes connections with King George 3rd who used The Hall (then a private house) as a retreat during his bouts of madness. The Hall is now the Raven Hall Hotel and was built in 1774 over the remains of a Roman signal station, one of a chain along the east coast.

Alum mining was prominent on this part of the coast in the 17th century. The old workings are being restored and are open for your inspection. There was also a brick company at Ravenscar. The old quarry and remains of the kilns can still be seen along the old railway line towards Robin Hoods Bay. The path leading to the line is paved in places with bricks bearing the Ravenscar Brick company's name.

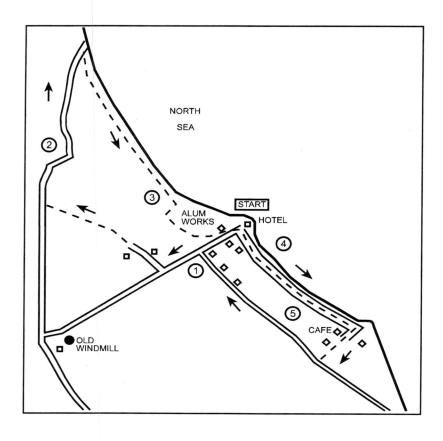

FACT FILE.
Distance - 8 miles (13km)
Time - 3 hours
Grading - Easy
Map - OS Landranger 94
Start - Plenty of roadside parking at Ravenscar
Grid Reference - 980015

THE ROUTE
1. Start from the Raven Hall Hotel at Ravenscar and walk back along the road you came on. Continue past the telephone box then turn right at the bridleway sign along Robin Hood Lane. Keep to the track straight ahead when the road expires near the bungalow on the left.

2. Where the track forks keep straight on. Eventually you will meet the Stoupe Brow road, bear right here and continue downhill all the way to Stoupe Brow Cottage Farm, and enjoy the superb scenery.

3. Take the sign for the Cleveland Way on the right near the old war relic on the coast and use the cliff path towards Ravenscar. The path winds its way along the cliff top then swerves inland to join a wider path to pass the sign for the Alum Works. The works are worth a look, there are a few ruins and an information board explaining the site.

4. Follow the yellow arrow through the woods on the right then keep left each time the path forks to return to the Raven Hall Hotel. Walk past the hotel keeping it on your left past the wire fence. Where the fence ends take the Cleveland Way sign to return to the cliff path.

5. In a little over a mile cross the stile on the right at the public footpath sign across the field to a stone stile. At the road turn right back towards Ravenscar. At the 'T' junction turn right again to take you back to the start and possibly a cup of tea. Me? I think I'll have a dip in the hotel swimming pool!

If you visit the alum works look out to sea and try to imagine the flat bottomed ships bringing in their stinking cargo of urine collected form public houses in London and Hull. The urine was mixed with alum shale to help to crystallise it. Most of the land you have walked on belongs to the National Trust. Perhaps you noticed the National Trust Centre at the start of the walk, please give them your support.

ROUTE 7

THE JUGGER HOWE JOGGLE

The walk over Stoney Marl Moor and Jugger Howe Moor can be exposed in bad weather, go prepared! Jugger Howe was a military training area with connections over the moor to Low North Camp at Harwood Dale. The army had a practice firing range on Jugger Howe after the last war but the land has now been returned to agriculture and sheep farming.

- - - o 0 o - - -

FACT FILE
Distance - 8 miles (13km)
Time - 3 hours
Grading - Moderate
Map - OS Landranger 94. OS Outdoor Leisure 27
Start - Ravenscar
Grid Reference - 980015
Refreshments - Raven Hall Hotel and a small cafe at Ravenscar

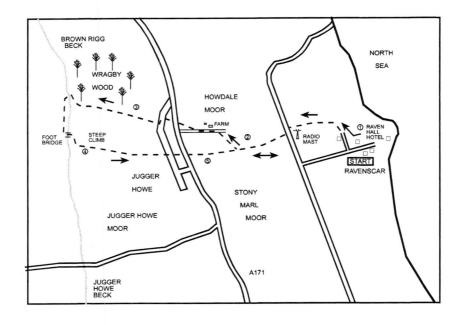

THE ROUTE

1. This trek begins at Ravenscar perched on the 600ft cliffs high above the North Sea situated between Scarborough and Whitby. There is ample parking as marked on the roadside. Start with the Raven Hall Hotel at your back and walk uphill along the road you arrived on in a westerly direction for about a quarter of a mile. Turn right at the bridleway sign along Robin Hood Lane. Keep straight ahead at the end of the road up a rough track following the bridleway sign. Shortly the track forks, take the track to the left and follow the yellow arrow to the road and radio mast.

2. At the radio mast turn right onto the moor at the bridleway sign opposite. In one mile the track splits, take the bridleway marked with a blue arrow to the right. Follow this to the farm road then turn left still following the sign for the bridleway. After a corner look out on your right for a gate with a blue arrow on it. Turn right here and cross the field diagonally right. Shortly you will reach a gate onto the main road, the busy A171. Cross with care then follow a path across the verge keeping the gorse on your left you soon meet an old road. Go left here then in 100yards go right over a stile into the meadow.

3. Follow the yellow arrow now keeping close to the line of a fence on your right. Cross a stile bearing right and eventually the path drops down into Wragby Wood to a junction of becks. Follow the path around to the right then when the path splits bear left over a wooden bridge. Follow the path round straight on now following the line of Jugger Howe Beck on your left.

4. It is rough terrain now and boggy at times but keep following the line of the beck until you arrive at a footbridge. Cross the bridge over Jugger Howe Beck then follow the yellow arrow to the right then round to the left and climb steeply up the end of the Rigg. Almost a scramble! At the top continue straight ahead to meet an old concrete army road.

5. The old road takes you over Jugger Howe Moor to meet the A171 again. Cross the busy road with care and continue along the footpath opposite to climb onto Stony Marl Moor and Howdale Moor to aim for the radio mast in the distance. At the mast cross the road to follow the public footpath sign to take you back to Ravenscar.

19

ROUTE 8

A SCARBOROUGH HISTORICAL TOUR
(Don't lose your head on this walk, Piers did!)

*S*carborough, gem of the east coast. Queen of watering places. Britain's number one seaside resort. Well I would say that I'm a Scarborian!
There is no better place for a walk on a still summer's evening with the sun setting over the moor giving a magi-

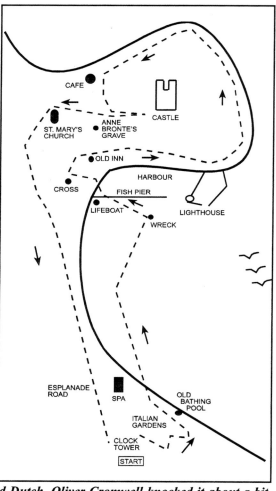

cal glow to the headland and castle. Steeped in history Bronze Age man through Romans, Vikings and Normans. It all started in 966 when that wily Viking, Thorgils Skarthi raided the town. He decided it was a good place to settle and called the place Scardeburg. In 1066 the blood thirsty Harald Hardrada came and burnt the town. Before the Vikings the Romans were here! Around 370AD They built a miniature fortification on the headland called a signal station to warn of impending raiders along the coast. But it wasn't until the Norman conquest that the first real fortifications were built on the headland and it evolved into the castle that we know today. Early in the 12th century William le Gros built a gate tower and curtain wall, but the keep wasn't erected until the 1160's under the orders of Henry 2nd. Although it had its share of troubles. It was attacked by the French, Scots and Dutch. Oliver Cromwell knocked it about a bit, but it was the might of the German Navy during the first world war that did the most damage by shelling the town and castle as they raided the east coast. Take a walk with me one balmy summer's evening along the coast and find out about some more of Scarborough's secrets.

Distance - 3½ miles (5km)
Time - 3 hours
Grading - Easy
Map - OS Landranger 101
Start - Scarborough South Cliff.
Grid Ref. 048873
Refreshments - Try the famous Scarborough ice cream or have a delicious meal of Fish & Chips

THE ROUTE

I'll start the walk from the Clock Tower adjacent to the putting green on the Esplanade on the South Cliff, but you can choose a different starting point anywhere along the route if it is more convenient to you. Go under the arches of the Clock Tower turning left then right to join the paths which zig-zag down the cliff to the promenade. From the swimming pool head along the promenade towards the Spa.

This magnificent building, started life as a Spa house but was frequently washed into the sea, and in 1737 a cliff fall obliterated the springs. The springs forced their way out again some months later and a new spa house was built. They were discovered by a Mrs. Farrow, who by her own experience pronounced they contained minerals to help the cure of most illnesses. The ingredients of the water are mainly magnesium and lime with a little iron and natron thrown in for good luck. I cannot vouch for their medicinal properties but I'll wager they would aid certain bodily functions!

Leave the Spa behind you now and walk on the beach if the tide is out. If not stay on the promenade.

Imagine the scene along the waters edge in the 18th century for it was around this time that sea bathing was 'invented'. Gentlemen would jump into the sea naked from a boat a respectful distance from the shore, whilst ladies, who of course averted their eyes from such bawdy goings on, demurely changed their attire in bathing machines at the waters edge. Near the harbour you might see the remains of a shipwreck in the sand which occasionally appears.

Head for the lifeboat house now to drop a coin in the collecting box before passing the west pier and the small huts selling all kinds of sea food. Cross the road at the traffic lights and walk up Eastborough. In a few yards at a sharp bend go straight ahead along West Sandgate following the sign for Old Town, Castle and St. Mary's Church. Soon you will see on your left the remains of the old Buttercross. You are now in Princess Square, turn right here into Princess St. and at the end right again. At Burr Bank follow the road right then left. At the bottom of the hill turn left along Quay Street.

In this part of the town there are many strange street names. Look out for these - The Bolts, Long Greece Steps, Bethel Place, Tuthill, Bakehouse Steps, Dog & Duck Lane, and Salmon Steps. Look up as you walk along Quay Street and you will see the remains of the old warehouses with their rotting jibs. Let your imagination run riot and visualise what it must have been like in the bustling days of sail along the quayside.

ROUTE 8 CONTINUED

The pale blue building on the right is the Three Mariners Inn, entrance round the front. It was built about 1300AD on the quayside and is a unique example of a typical waterside inn. It is believed to have had an underground entrance from the quayside into the cellar, an ideal way for illegal goods to be brought ashore. The Inn is intriguing in the fact that it has a secret bunk room hidden behind panelling. There are twenty six cupboards some with secret entrances. The one behind the fireplace even had a rope ladder to the cellar! You can visit the Three Mariners Inn for yourself, it is open to the public during the summer months.

At the end of Quay Street cross the road and head towards the harbour and lighthouse on the pier.

The harbour at Scarborough was important to the Vikings as it was used as a trade route from Scandinavia to York, Dublin and the Isle of Man. During the 13th century harbour trade boomed as stone and building materials were imported, wool was exported and it supported a growing fishing industry. In the 14th and 15th centuries trade continued to expand serving merchants from France, Spain, Ireland, Flanders the Mediterranean Ports, Norway and the Baltic. Unfortunately all this trade came to the notice of Pirates! They would lay in wait off the coast and attack the ships. The boom lasted until the 16th century when trade declined and it became mainly a fishing port. In the 18th century Scarborough again emerged as a profitable ship building port and coastal trader. Today a little trade is done by merchant ships but fishing is prominent at Scarborough, although with the quota system it seems to be in decline. Could the port be due for another change? The first lighthouse was built in 1806 and was lit by six tallow candles. In 1844 a keepers house and a second story with cupola and copper reflector was added. In 1914 it was shelled by the German Navy and damaged so badly it had to be destroyed. The one you see today was built and paid for by local people in 1931.

Leave the pier and walk round the Marine Drive. This feat of engineering took 10 years, 10 months and 10 days to complete to 1908. When you reach the Albert Drive Cafe on the left walk along the paths which zig zag up the cliff to the castle. Enter the castle grounds to spend time exploring. Bear in mind if you go in the evening that the

ghost of the headless Piers Gaveston, who once ran the castle but was beheaded by the Barons, walks the walls at dusk! Leave the castle to pay a visit to St. Mary's Church and ruins, but before doing so pay homage to the grave of Anne Bronte in the cemetery. Pass the church on your left along Castle Rd. then turn left along Tollergate into Friargate and visit the old Market Hall at the bottom. Continue into Eastborough, turn right then left into King Street. At the end of King Street turn left past the lift, down the steps onto Marine Parade and exit into St. Nicholas Cliff. Walk past the Grand Hotel to cross the Spa Bridge. Turn right then sharp left up the steps at the end of the bridge to take you back onto the Esplanade and eventually the Clock Tower.

BEMPTON BIRD SANCTUARY

If you have time why not include this visit to the bird sanctuary with your walk round Flamborough Head? You could start from North Landing and take the cliff path north. Otherwise it makes an interesting half day or evening interlude to your walking holiday. Only a short walk but worth a visit to see the only nesting colony of Gannets in England. You will also see Puffins, Terns, Guillemots, Razorbills and many other sea birds vying for territory on the cliffs. Viewing areas are provided by the R.S.P.B. on the cliff edge. Anyone frightened of heights should give this one a miss as the 300ft cliffs fall sheer to the rocks below.

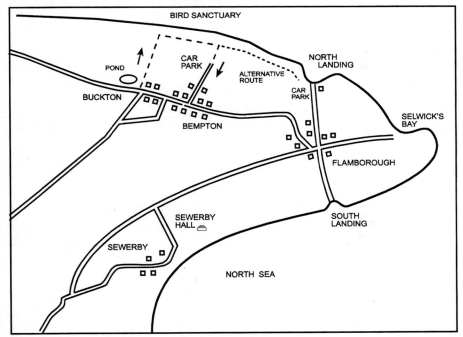

THE ROUTE

Approach Bempton from the A165 or the B1229 or take the minor roads as signed from Bridlington. Turn off down the side of the White Horse pub along Cliff Lane. At the end of the lane use the car park provided. There is lots of information at the R.S.P.B. centre on the way to the viewing gantry's. If you fancy a walk before visiting the bird sanctuary, return on the road to Bempton turning right at the pub to walk along to the village of Buckton. Pass through Buckton and at the duck pond turn right along Hoddy Cows Lane following the sign to Buckton Cliffs. In 1½ miles turn right to visit the bird sanctuary viewing points then return to your car. If you do not wish to walk to the village simply walk to the cliffs and visit the various viewing points provided, and I hope you have a good head for heights!

ROUTE 10

FLAMBOROUGH HEAD

*K*nown as 'The Bermuda Triangle' by many people because of the weather which can be most peculiar at this point on the coast. One minute an enveloping sea mist rolls onto the head when all around is in brilliant sunshine. Or sometimes a violent squall will blow in from the sea when you are least expecting it. However, because of the shape of the headland there is always a sheltered bay to be found. The main places of interest are Thornwick Bay and North Landing on the north face, Selwicks Bay on the headland point and South Landing on the south side.

FACT FILE

Distance - 9 miles (15km)
Time - 3½ hours
Grading - Easy
Map - OS Landranger 101
Start - North Landing Flamborough
Grid Reference - 239720
Refreshments - Sewerby and
North Landing

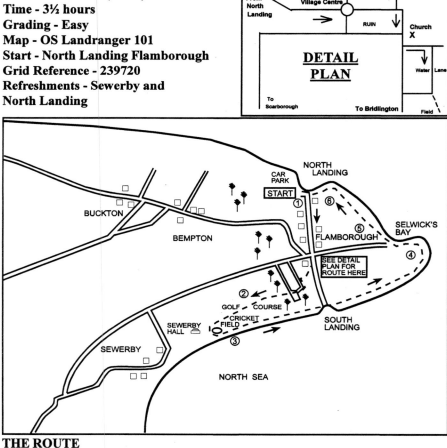

THE ROUTE

1. Start from the car park at North Landing, Flamborough. Walk along the road into Flamborough following signs for Bridlington. Keep on through the village then take the first turn left past the church, shortly turning right into Water Lane.

2. At the first corner turn left over the stile into a field, signed to Danes Dyke. Keep on the path which eventually leads to a narrow road. Turn left at the road along the footpath towards Danes Dyke car park. At Danes Dyke where the road goes left towards the car park (*there are toilets in the car park*) go straight ahead across the road onto a narrow bridleway alongside a brick wall then down steep steps into the Dyke. Cross the footbridge and head up the other side bearing left at the top. In a few yards take the signed path to Sewerby on the right. This goes across the golf course, please keep to the path provided.

3. At Sewerby walk along the side of the cricket field. If you wish to visit Sewerby Hall and grounds the entrance is on the right. If it is refreshment you require continue along into the village. If you only came for the walk go left around the cricket field to the cliff top and turn left again to take the cliff path towards Flamborough Head.

4. It is an arduous journey along the cliff path as it rises and falls following the contours of the cliffs, but there is the opportunity for a paddle at South Landing! The cliff path is well maintained with steps fabricated in the side of the cliff. Selwicks Bay is probably the most interesting part of the walk for it is here that we find not one, but two lighthouses!

5. *The old 'chalk tower' lighthouse was built around 1674 from the local chalk. Its light source was a brazier which was lit at the top of the tower. It is possible it was never even used, opinions vary. The modern lighthouse was built in 1806 and was completed by a local builder who constructed the 90 odd foot tower without using any scaffolding! No matter how many lighthouses there are they are all rendered useless by a good old fashioned sea fog. The building on the cliff top a few hundred yards from the lighthouse is a fog horn. Stand near it on a foggy day and clear your sinuses!*

6. After visiting the lighthouses return to the cliff path following signs for North Landing. You will probably notice the sea becoming a little more choppy now. Look out for the sea birds nesting in the cliffs as you approach North Landing they are a most intriguing sight. Follow the cliff path back to the car park but not without first visiting the caves on the beach.

At low tide the caves are accessible for exploration but they were used for a more sinister purpose years ago. Smuggling! Flamborough had a famous smuggler called Robin Lythe. He was found in a cave and named Robin after the fisherman who found him. Robin Lythe's cave can be seen at the right hand side of the cove and can be entered at low water. Enjoy the grounds of Sewerby Hall if you have time and the Hall itself is worth exploring. Visit the lighthouses at Selwicks Bay. When looking south see if you can pick out the sweep of Spurn Point, it projects an unbelievable distance out to sea.

25

ROUTE 11 - QUICKIE
3 MILES

THE HAYBURN HOBBLE

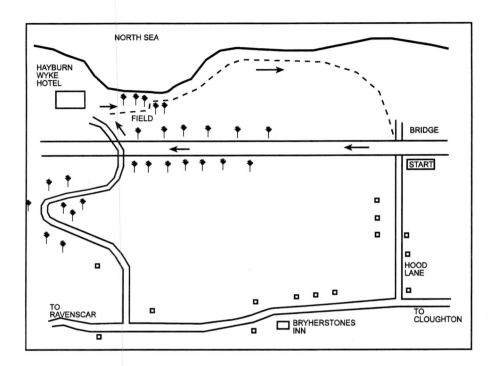

THE ROUTE

At Cloughton on the A171 Scarborough to Whitby road just past the Red Lion pub turn right towards Ravenscar. In half a mile turn right along Hood Lane and park on the grass verge near the bridge. Please park respectfully - do not prevent field access - park well away from the houses - by the bridge would be fine.

Walk onto the old railway line at the bridge and turn left in a northerly direction.

In 1 mile you arrive at a gate. Turn right along the road to the Hayburn Wyke Hotel, an old coaching inn. The name Hayburn Wyke means 'hunting enclosure by a stream'. On a pleasant summers evening sit outside and have a well earned pint. Leave the Hotel the same way as you arrived but this time take the path angled off to the left. At the field cross the stile keeping left to another stile opposite into the wood. If you wish to visit the waterfall keep straight on to the shore then return to this point. If not look out for a path uphill through the trees to the right leading to the cliff top footpath.

The walk back along the cliff is enhanced by fabulous views along the Heritage Coast towards Scarborough and Flamborough. In a little over a mile take the path leaving the cliffs on the right to return to Hood Lane.

26

ROUTE 12 - QUICKIE
2 MILES

FILEY BRIGG
A low tide walk

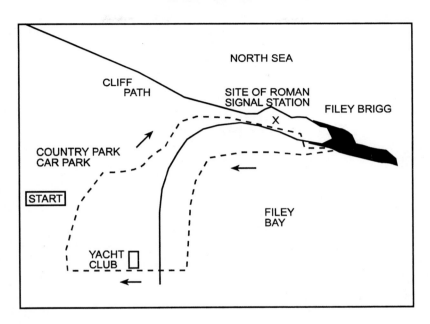

THE ROUTE

Be wary of the tide, do not go onto the Brigg if the sea is washing over or advancing.

Make your way to the North Cliff Country Park car park at Filey. It is well signed from the town, when you arrive drive to the farthest point on the park. You will see the promontory of the Brigg reaching out into the sea. Start the walk along the cliff above the Brigg. About half way along there are steps built into the side of the cliff on the right, do not proceed any further along the cliff top, it is dangerous. Use the steps provided which take you onto the sea shore. Keep straight ahead with the cliff on your left as you walk along the route of the sewer pipe to the rocky remains of the Brigg. One of the large pools formed in the rocks was said to have been used by a Roman Emperor for bathing!

On the Brigg there is a new aspect to Filey as you stand way out in Filey Bay looking across to the high cliffs of Flamborough Head. In the north the view is to Scarborough. Quite an impressive sight with the castle on the headland towering over the old town beneath. Retrace your steps and this time do not take the path to the cliff top but remain on the beach and return to the car park via the Filey Yacht Club road further along the bay on the right.

27

TRAILBLAZER BOOKS

CYCLING BOOKS
Mountain Biking around the Yorkshire Dales
Mountain Biking the Easy Way
Mountain Biking in North Yorkshire
Mountain Biking on the Yorkshire Wolds
Mountain Biking for Pleasure
Mountain Biking in the Lake District
Mountain Biking around Ryedale, Wydale & the North York Moors
Exploring Ryedale, Moor & Wold by Bicycle
Beadle's Bash - 100 mile challenge route for Mountain Bikers

WALKING BOOKS
Walking the Riggs & Ridges of the North York Moors
Short Walks around the Yorkshire Coast
Walking on the Yorkshire Coast
Walking to Abbeys, Castles & Churches
Walking around the North York Moors
Walking around Scarborough, Whitby & Filey
Walking to Crosses on the North York Moors
Walks from the Harbour
Walking in Dalby, the Great Yorkshire Forest

THE SCENIC WALKS SERIES
Ten Scenic Walks around Rosedale, Farndale & Hutton le Hole
Twelve Scenic Walks from the North Yorkshire Moors Railway
Twelve Scenic Walks around the Yorkshire Dales
Twelve Scenic Walks around Ryedale, Pickering & Helmsley

THE POCKET BOOK SERIES
The Crucial Guide to the Yorkshire Coast
The Crucial Guide to Ryedale & North York Moors
The Crucial Guide to York & District
The Crucial Guide to Crosses & Stones on the North York Moors

DOING IT YOURSELF SERIES
Make & Publish Your Own Books

THE EXPLORER SERIES
Exploring Ryedale, Moor & Wold by Bicycle

YORKSHIRE BOOKS
Curious Goings on in Yorkshire

For more information please visit our web site:
www.trailblazerbooks.co.uk